D1126791

The McMahons

Vince McMahon
and Family

by Angie Peterson Kaelberer

Reading Consultant:
Dr. Robert Miller
Professor of Special Education
Minnesota State University, Mankato

CAPSTONE
HIGH-INTEREST
BOOKS

an imprint of Capstone Press
Mankato, Minnesota

Capstone High-Interest Books are published by Capstone Press
151 Good Counsel Drive, P.O. Box 669, Mankato, Minnesota 56002
http://www.capstone-press.com

Library of Congress Cataloging-in-Publication Data
Kaelberer, Angie Peterson.
    The McMahons: Vince McMahon and family / by Angie Peterson Kaelberer.
    p. cm.—(Pro wrestlers)
    Includes bibliographical references and index.
    Summary: Traces the life and career of the professional wrestling promoter
whose family has been in the professional wrestling business for more than
eighty years.
    ISBN 0-7368-2143-0 (hardcover)
    1. McMahon, Vince—Juvenile literature. 2. Wrestlers—United States—
Biography—Juvenile literature. [1. McMahon, Vince. 2. Wrestlers.] I. Title: Vince
McMahon and family. II. Title. III. Series.
GV1196.M43K34 2004
796.812'092—dc21   2003007646

Editorial Credits
Karen Risch, product planning editor; Timothy Halldin, series designer;
    Patrick Dentinger, book designer; Jo Miller, photo researcher

Photo Credits
AP/Wide World Photos/Mark Lennihan, 29
Corbis/Duomo, 4, 7; Sygma/Jason Szenes, 8; Jacques M. Chenet, 18
Dr. Michael Lano, 13, 21, 22, 25
Getty Images/Lawrence Lucier, 10; Steven Henry, 14; Spencer Platt, 30;
    Tom Hauck, 34; Liaison/Arnaldo Magnani, 42
Michael Blair, cover (all), 16, 26, 32, 36, 39, 41

1 2 3 4 5 6 08 07 06 05 04 03

Capstone Press thanks Dr. Michael Lano, WReaLano@aol.com, for his assistance in the
preparation of this book.

Table of Contents

Chapter 1

An Owner and a Champion

On September 14, 1999, pro wrestling fans filled the Thomas and Mack Center in Las Vegas, Nevada. The fans were there to cheer for the World Wrestling Federation (WWF) wrestlers as they taped the *Smackdown!* TV show.

Near the end of the night, Paul Levesque walked into the ring. Levesque wrestles as Triple H. Triple H was the WWF World Champion. He had promised to allow another wrestler to challenge him for the title. The fans did not know who that wrestler would be.

Vince McMahon is the owner of World Wrestling Entertainment.

The fans were surprised when Triple H asked WWF owner Vince McMahon to wrestle him for the championship. Vince was not a wrestler, but he agreed to meet Triple H in the ring. Triple H asked Vince's son, Shane, to be the referee for the match.

An Unusual Match

Few fans expected Vince to win. Vince was in good shape, but he was nearly 25 years older than Triple H. Also, wrestler Joanie Laurer was at ringside to help Triple H. Laurer was known as Chyna.

Triple H began the match by punching and choking Vince. Vince jumped out of the ring. Triple H followed him. Triple H choked Vince with a cable. He then shoved Vince down on the announcer's table. Triple H climbed on the fence that separated the fans from the ring. He used an elbow drop to put Vince through the announcer's table. Triple H then threw Vince back into the ring.

Chyna handed a chair to Triple H. Shane tried to help Vince. Triple H pushed Shane away and slammed Vince with the chair.

Vince accepted Triple H's challenge to wrestle for the World Championship.

Shane then speared Triple H to the mat. Chyna ran into the ring. She and Triple H knocked Shane to the mat.

Vince's wife, Linda, then ran into the ring to help her husband and son. Chyna grabbed Linda and held her back as Triple H pounded Vince. Triple H then tried to take Vince down with a Pedigree. Triple H held Vince face down between his legs. Triple H prepared to drop to his knees and slam Vince to the mat.

In 2000, the McMahons celebrated the WWF becoming part of the New York Stock Exchange (NYSE). NYSE Chairman Richard Grasso is in the center of the photo.

Just then, Steve Williams ran into the ring. Williams wrestles as "Stone Cold" Steve Austin. Austin took Chyna down with a Stone Cold Stunner. Austin stood in front of Chyna and wrapped his arm around her head. He then dropped to his knees, slamming Chyna to the mat.

Austin followed his first Stone Cold Stunner with one for Triple H. As Triple H lay on the mat,

Austin dragged Vince on top of him. Austin then helped Shane get up. Shane counted to three. At age 54, Vince had beaten Triple H to become the WWF World Champion. Vince was the first non-wrestler in WWF history to hold the title.

About the McMahons

The McMahon family has been in the pro wrestling business for more than 80 years. In the 1920s, Vince's grandfather, Jess McMahon, put on professional boxing and wrestling matches in New York City. In 1935, Jess's son, Vincent J. McMahon, joined his father in the business. In 1963, Vincent changed the company's name to the World Wide Wrestling Federation (WWWF). In 1982, Vincent's son Vince bought the company from his father. Vince changed the company's name to the World Wrestling Federation (WWF).

In 2002, the company changed its name again. Today, it is called World Wrestling Entertainment (WWE). Vince, Linda, and their children, Shane and Stephanie, all work for WWE.

Chapter 2

The Early Years

Vincent Kennedy McMahon was born August 24, 1945, in Pinehurst, North Carolina. His parents, Vincent J. and Vicki, met and married during World War II (1939–1945). At the time, Vincent J. was serving with the U.S. Coast Guard in North Carolina.

Vincent and Vicki divorced soon after Vince was born. Vincent moved to Washington, D.C., to start a wrestling company called Capitol Wrestling. Vincent later changed the company's name to the World Wide Wrestling Federation.

In the early days of pro wrestling, each part of the country had its own promoter. These promoters put on matches only in their area,

Vince was born in Pinehurst, North Carolina.

which was called their territory. Vincent soon controlled the Northeast territory.

Vicki remained in North Carolina with young Vince and his older brother, Rodney. Vicki married a man named Leo Lupton. The family lived near Havelock, North Carolina.

Vince's early childhood was hard. His father never visited. Vince did not get along with his stepfather. Vince also had trouble in school. He had a learning disability called dyslexia that made reading very difficult.

A Better Life

In 1957, Vincent came to Havelock to visit his sons. The boys began spending summers with their father and his new wife, Juanita.

Vince and Rodney went with their father to wrestling matches in Washington, D.C., and New York City. Vince loved the exciting world of wrestling. He watched the matches and hung around the wrestlers outside the ring. He dreamed of joining his father in the wrestling business when he grew up.

Vincent did not want his sons in the wrestling business. He wanted them to go to college. When Vince was 14, his father sent

Vince McMahon's Hero: "Dr." Jerry Graham

As a teenager, Vince met many of the WWWF's top wrestlers. His favorite wrestler was "Dr." Jerry Graham.

Graham was 6 feet, 3 inches (191 centimeters) tall. He weighed about 300 pounds (136 kilograms) during his top wrestling years.

Graham was born in 1929 in Phoenix, Arizona. At age 14, he started wrestling. In the 1950s, Graham teamed with Eddie Gossett to form the Golden Grahams tag team. Gossett wrestled as Eddie Graham. The Golden Grahams won several U.S. Tag Team titles.

In the 1970s, Graham trained young wrestlers and still wrestled occasionally. Graham died January 24, 1997. He was 68 years old.

Vince has been married to Linda Edwards since 1966.

him to Fishburne Military School in
Waynesboro, Virginia. At Fishburne, Vince
played football and was on the wrestling team.

When Vince was 16, he met 13-year-old
Linda Edwards. Linda and Vince began dating.
When Vince was home from school, he spent
most of his time with Linda and her family
in Havelock.

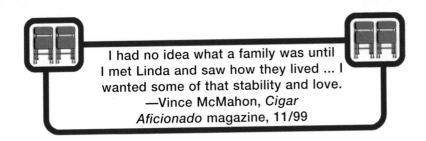

I had no idea what a family was until I met Linda and saw how they lived ... I wanted some of that stability and love.
—Vince McMahon, *Cigar Aficionado* magazine, 11/99

College and Marriage

Vince graduated from Fishburne in 1964. He began classes at East Carolina University in Greenville, North Carolina. Two years later, Linda graduated from Havelock High School. On August 6, 1966, Vince and Linda were married in Havelock.

Linda joined Vince at East Carolina University. In May 1969, Vince received a degree in marketing. Linda earned a degree in French.

Linda and Vince moved to Washington, D.C. Vince found a job in sales, but he had not forgotten about the wrestling business. Six months later, Vince's father called him. Vincent offered Vince a job as a ring announcer. Vince started announcing matches on the WWWF's TV show, *All-Star Wrestling*. He was happy to be working with his father.

On January 15, 1970, Linda and Vince became parents. Shane Brandon McMahon was born in Gaithersburg, Maryland.

Vince and Linda's daughter, Stephanie, was born in 1976. Today, she works for WWE.

A New Opportunity

By 1971, TV stations in 14 states were showing *All-Star Wrestling*. Vincent moved the tapings of the TV show to larger theaters in Hamburg and Allentown, Pennsylvania. Every three weeks, Vincent, Vince, and the wrestlers traveled to Pennsylvania for the shows.

In 1972, Vincent put Vince in charge of a wrestling operation in Bangor, Maine. Vince,

Linda, and Shane moved to West Hartford, Connecticut. Each weekend, Vince drove to Bangor for the matches. After expenses, he sometimes made only $50 each night.

In September 1976, Vince and Linda had a daughter, Stephanie. Vince knew he needed to make more money to provide for his growing family. In 1979, he began renting the Cape Cod Coliseum in South Yarmouth, Massachusetts. Vince put on wrestling matches and hockey games in the arena. Vince moved his family to South Yarmouth. Every three weeks, he returned to Pennsylvania for *All-Star Wrestling*.

Taking Over the Business

Vincent retired in 1982. He offered to sell the WWWF to Vince. Vince borrowed money from several banks for a down payment. He told his father he would pay off the rest of the price over the next two years.

Vince also made another promise to his father. Vincent asked Vince to respect the territories of the other wrestling promoters. He did not want Vince to put the other promoters out of business. Vince agreed, but it was a promise he did not keep.

Chapter 3

The WWF

Vince made some changes soon after he took over the WWWF. He changed the company's name to the World Wrestling Federation (WWF). He moved the company's offices to Stamford, Connecticut. He also hired a wrestler who would become the sport's biggest name in the 1980s. That wrestler was Terry Bollea, who wrestles as Hulk Hogan.

Hogan had wrestled for the WWWF once before, starting in 1979. In 1982, Hogan quit after Vincent refused to give him time off to act in the movie *Rocky III.*

Vince's idea to hire Hogan was a good one. Hogan quickly became popular with the fans.

In 1984, Vince hired Hulk Hogan, who quickly became the WWF's top wrestler.

Many people came to WWF shows to see him. They also bought Hogan T-shirts, toys, and magazines. The sale of those products made the WWF a great deal of money. Soon, Vince started selling these products for his other top wrestlers.

Going National

Before the 1980s, most wrestling TV shows were shown only in the part of the country where they were taped. Vince started buying time on TV stations all over the country for the WWF's shows. The other wrestling promoters became angry with Vince, but he did not care. He wanted the WWF to reach wrestling fans all over the United States.

By the early 1980s, many homes in the United States had cable TV. Vince wanted to get the WWF's shows on a major cable TV station. In late 1983, Vince signed a contract with the USA Network. At that time, this cable station reached about 24 million homes. The next year, Vince got his shows on the Turner Broadcasting System (TBS) network. Ted Turner owned this large cable station in Atlanta, Georgia. Soon, the WWF was producing five TV shows each week.

In the 1980s, Andre the Giant and Hulk Hogan
wrestled some great matches for the WWF.

In early 1984, Vince's father became sick
with cancer. He died May 27, 1984. Vincent's
death made Vince want to make the WWF even
more successful.

WrestleMania
Late in 1984, Vince had another idea. He
wanted to put on the biggest event pro
wrestling fans had ever seen. He wanted it

At WrestleMania 3, Davey Boy Smith (top) wrestled Bret Hart.

to be as popular with wrestling fans as the Super Bowl is with football fans. He decided to call it WrestleMania.

On March 31, 1985, about 22,000 fans filled Madison Square Garden in New York City for WrestleMania. Nearly 400,000 more fans around the country paid to watch the show on closed-circuit TV. WrestleMania earned Vince and the WWF about $4 million.

Vince was happy with WrestleMania's success. He decided to hold another WrestleMania the next year. The matches took place at three arenas. The arenas were in New York, Illinois, and California. People in other parts of the country watched on closed-circuit TV or in their own homes on pay-per-view. These people rented a device from their cable TV company that allowed them to view the show. Much of the WWF's earnings from the show came from pay-per-view customers.

The next year, Vince decided to hold WrestleMania at the Pontiac Silverdome in Pontiac, Michigan. This huge stadium held 93,000 people. On March 29, 1987, a sold-out crowd watched Hulk Hogan pin Andre "the Giant" Roussimoff in the main event. The size of the crowd set a world record for an indoor sporting event. The WWF made more than $11 million from the show.

Movies and More

The success of WrestleMania gave Vince an idea about how to increase the WWF's audience. He decided the company should produce a movie starring Hulk Hogan.

The WWF spent $20 million to make *No Holds Barred*. The movie came out in May 1989. It did not do well. The WWF lost millions of dollars on the movie.

Vince was disappointed by the movie's failure, but he still wanted to find other ways to reach sports fans. Besides WrestleMania, he produced three pay-per-view TV events each year. These events were SummerSlam, Survivor Series, and the Royal Rumble.

In 1990, Vince decided to produce a TV show for professional bodybuilders. These athletes develop their muscles by lifting weights, exercising, and eating healthy foods. They often compete at bodybuilding contests.

Vince hired 13 bodybuilders to compete for the World Bodybuilding Federation (WBF). In June 1991, the WBF held its first bodybuilding contest in Atlantic City, New Jersey. Each month, the bodybuilders also appeared in a show on TBS called *Body Stars*.

The WBF was not a success. It held just one more contest before Vince shut down the company in July 1992. The WWF lost about $15 million on the WBF.

In the late 1990s, The Rock and "Stone Cold" Steve Austin helped make *Raw* popular with wrestling fans.

Vince decided to concentrate on wrestling after the failure of the movie and the WBF. In January 1993, the WWF began producing a new TV show called *Monday Night Raw*. The show quickly became popular, but the WWF's problems were not over. Another wrestling company was determined to put the WWF out of business. That company was World Championship Wrestling (WCW).

Chapter 4

Challenge and Success

In 1988, TBS owner Ted Turner bought the National Wrestling Alliance (NWA). In 1991, he changed the company's name to World Championship Wrestling and moved it from North Carolina to Atlanta, Georgia.

Vince was a rich man, but Turner was even richer. He could afford to offer wrestlers more money than the WWF was paying them. In the early 1990s, many top WWF wrestlers took jobs with WCW. One of these wrestlers was Hulk Hogan.

Vince's battles with WCW began in the early 1990s.

On Trial

Vince had an even bigger problem than losing his wrestlers to WCW. In November 1993, Vince was charged with six counts of buying illegal drugs called steroids and giving them to his wrestlers. Steroids can cause the muscles to grow very large. They also can cause heart damage and death.

Vince said the charges were not true. At his trial, the judge dismissed five of the six charges because of lack of evidence. In July 1994, the jury found Vince not guilty of the sixth charge.

The trial had taken up most of Vince's time. He was eager to again spend his time on the WWF.

Monday Night Wrestling War

On September 4, 1995, WCW started showing a new wrestling TV show on TBS. It was called *Monday Nitro*. Each week, WCW broadcast the show live from a different city.

Every other week, the WWF taped two hours of *Monday Night Raw*. The first hour of

In July 1994, Vince and Linda left the courtroom after he was found not guilty of drug charges. Vince wore a neck brace due to a motorcycle accident.

the show aired live that night. The next hour was shown the following Monday. Soon, *Nitro* host Eric Bischoff started telling WCW viewers the endings of the WWF's taped matches. Many wrestling fans started watching *Nitro* instead of *Monday Night Raw*. Vince knew he had to change his show to compete with WCW.

Vince McMahon's Rival: Ted Turner

During the 1990s, the WWF's main rival was World Championship Wrestling. WCW's owner was Ted Turner.

Turner was born in 1938 in Cincinnati, Ohio. In 1971, he bought a TV station in Atlanta, Georgia. He 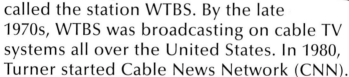 called the station WTBS. By the late 1970s, WTBS was broadcasting on cable TV systems all over the United States. In 1980, Turner started Cable News Network (CNN).

Turner got into the wrestling business in 1988 when he bought the NWA. In 1991, he changed the company's name to World Championship Wrestling.

In 1996, Turner sold Turner Broadcasting System to Time Warner Inc. In 2001, Time Warner merged with America Online. Officials at the new company sold WCW to Vince McMahon in March 2001. In 2001, Turner became vice chairman of AOL Time Warner. He held this position until he resigned in January 2003.

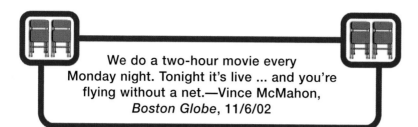

In November 1996, the USA Network started showing *Monday Night Raw* one hour later. The show aired at the same time that *Monday Nitro* aired.

Vince made other changes in the show as well. Until then, the WWF had aimed its shows mainly at children. Vince and the show's writers changed *Monday Night Raw* to make it more interesting to adults. The show's name changed to *Raw Is War*. The new show had more adult situations and language. In 1997, *Raw Is War* became a two-hour live show in a different city each week. Because the show was live, Bischoff could not give away its ending on *Nitro*.

Vince made other changes to bring fans back to the WWF. He hired new wrestlers. One of these wrestlers was Steve Austin. Austin quickly became one of the most popular wrestlers in WWF history. Vince also started to appear as himself on TV. Before, he had only appeared as an announcer on the

Vince and Linda's son, Shane, began wrestling for the WWF in 1998.

WWF's shows. He never told fans that he was the company's owner.

Now, Vince talked on TV about owning the company. He scheduled matches and argued with wrestlers on camera. He often argued with Austin. Fans liked to see a wrestler argue with his boss and win. More people started watching *Raw Is War*. Soon, it was beating *Nitro* in the TV ratings each week.

In May 1999, the WWF began another prime-time TV show. *WWF Smackdown!* was taped each Tuesday in a different city. It aired on the UPN TV network each Thursday.

A Family Business

Vince's family joined him in the WWF. Linda handled many of the WWF's business deals. As they grew up, Shane and Stephanie helped out by cleaning offices, answering phones, and setting up and taking down rings at matches.

In 1994, Shane graduated from Boston University with a communications degree. He began working full-time for the WWF as a TV producer. In 1998, he became an announcer on the WWF's new show, *Sunday Night Heat*. Later that year, he started appearing with Vince on *Raw Is War*.

Shane even wrestled a few matches. On February 15, 1999, he defeated Sean Waltman to win the WWF European Championship. Waltman wrestled as X-Pac.

Vince started the XFL in 2001.

Soon, the whole McMahon family was involved in the WWF. Stephanie started working full-time for the WWF after she graduated from Boston University in 1998. The next year, she joined Vince and Shane on the WWF's TV shows. Linda also sometimes appeared on the shows. As part of the storyline, the McMahons argued and fought with each other. Wrestling fans tuned in to see what the family would say and do next.

The XFL

In 2000, Vince got another idea. He knew many pro wrestling fans also liked other sports. He decided to start a new football league. The league would play during the National Football League's off-season. It would have different rules than NFL football. Vince named the league the XFL.

Vince took his idea to the NBC TV network. NBC agreed to show the games each Saturday night. They also gave Vince $100 million to start the XFL. The league had eight teams.

On February 3, 2001, about 10 million people watched the first XFL game on NBC. The next week, only about 5 million people watched the game. Each week, fewer people tuned in.

In May 2001, NBC said they would not show the next season's games on their network. Vince knew the league could not succeed without TV coverage. He decided to close down the XFL. The WWF lost about $36 million on the XFL.

Vince was disappointed with the XFL's failure. He turned his attention back to the WWF.

Chapter 5

The McMahons Today

By 2000, AOL Time Warner owned WCW, and the wrestling company was in trouble. Fewer and fewer people watched WCW's TV shows. The company kept losing money. AOL Time Warner decided to sell WCW, but the sale fell through.

Vince heard about the failed WCW sale. In March 2001, he paid $4.3 million for WCW. Wrestling fans watched the last *Nitro* show on March 26.

Shane appeared on WCW's last *Nitro* show.

Roster Split

After Vince bought WCW, many WCW wrestlers got jobs with the WWF. These people included Hulk Hogan, Richard Fliehr, Scott Hall, Kevin Nash, and Booker Huffman. Fliehr wrestles as Ric Flair. Huffman wrestles as Booker T. Around the same time, Extreme Championship Wrestling (ECW) went out of business. This wrestling company was based in Philadelphia, Pennsylvania. Several ECW wrestlers also joined the WWF.

The WWF's wrestlers had always appeared on both *Smackdown!* and *Raw*. The WWF wrestlers got fewer chances to be on TV after the WCW and ECW wrestlers joined the company. Many WWF fans were not happy with this change.

Vince decided to split the wrestlers into two groups. One group would wrestle only on *Raw*. The other group would appear only on *Smackdown!*. Vince believed this change would give all of the wrestlers more TV time. On March 25, 2002, Vince held a draft on *Raw* to split the wrestlers into two groups.

Vince made several changes in his company
during 2002.

A New Name

The roster split was not the only change for the
WWF in 2002. A group called the World
Wildlife Fund sued the WWF over the use of
the initials "WWF." A court in the United
Kingdom ruled in favor of the World
Wildlife Fund.

> You have to live it [the wrestling business] in order to make it work. But it's something that I love to live.—Vince McMahon, *Dallas Morning News*, 1/7/03

Instead of fighting the decision, Vince and Linda decided to change their company's name. On May 6, 2002, the WWF became World Wrestling Entertainment Inc. (WWE).

The McMahon Family

Today, Vince and Linda live in a large home in Greenwich, Connecticut. They have a bullmastiff dog named Ruckus.

WWE takes up nearly all of Vince's time. For fun, he likes to ride motorcycles and go to movies with Linda.

Since 1998, Shane has been president of the company's new media department. He manages WWE's Internet sites. He sometimes appears on WWE's TV shows. Shane and his wife, Marissa, live in Greenwich.

Stephanie is the *Smackdown!* general manager and appears on the show nearly every week. Stephanie also lives in Greenwich.

Stephanie is the *Smackdown!* general manager. She often appears on TV with Vince.

Vince is still a very rich man. He could afford to never work again, but he says that he loves the wrestling business. His job does not seem like work to him. With both Shane and Stephanie in the business, the McMahon family will continue to be involved in pro wrestling for many years to come.

Career Highlights

1945—Vincent K. McMahon is born August 24 in North Carolina.

1970—Vince begins working as an announcer for *All-Star Wrestling*.

1972—Vince takes over a promotion in Maine.

1982—Vince buys the WWWF from his father and changes the company's name to the World Wrestling Federation.

1985—The WWF holds the first WrestleMania.

1994—Shane McMahon graduates from Boston University and joins the WWF full-time.

1998—Stephanie McMahon graduates from Boston University and joins the WWF full-time.

1999—Vince defeats Triple H to become the WWF World Champion.

2001—Vince starts the XFL and buys WCW; he closes the XFL later that year.

2002—The WWF changes its name to World Wrestling Entertainment Inc.

Words to Know

announcer (uh-NOUN-sur)—a person who describes the action during a sports event

arena (uh-REE-nuh)—a large building used for sports or entertainment events

draft (DRAFT)—the process of choosing a person to join a sports organization or team

dyslexia (diss-LEK-see-uh)—a learning disability that causes people to see letters in the wrong order

promoter (pruh-MOH-tur)—a person who organizes events such as concerts and wrestling matches

referee (ref-uh-REE)—a person who makes sure athletes follow the rules of a sport

steroid (STER-oid)—an illegal drug that can increase a person's strength and athletic ability; steroids can cause heart problems and death.

territory (TER-uh-tor-ee)—an area controlled by one wrestling promoter

To Learn More

Alexander, Kyle. *Vince McMahon Jr.* Pro Wrestling Legends. Philadelphia: Chelsea House, 2001.

Burgan, Michael. *Stone Cold: Pro Wrestler Steve Austin.* Pro Wrestlers. Mankato, Minn.: Capstone Press, 2002.

Hunter, Matt. *Pro Wrestling: The Early Years.* Pro Wrestling Legends. Philadelphia: Chelsea House, 2001.

Kaelberer, Angie Peterson. *Hulk Hogan: Pro Wrestler Terry Bollea.* Pro Wrestlers. Mankato, Minn.: Capstone Press, 2004.

Useful Addresses

**Professional Wrestling Hall of Fame
  & Museum**
P.O. Box 434
Latham, NY 12110

World Wrestling Entertainment Inc.
1241 East Main Street
Stamford, CT 06902

Internet Sites

Do you want to learn more about the McMahon family and about pro wrestling?
Visit the FactHound at *http://www.facthound.com*

FactHound can track down many sites to help you. All the FactHound sites are hand-selected by our editors. FactHound will fetch the best, most accurate information to answer your questions.

IT'S EASY! IT'S FUN!
1) Go to *http://www.facthound.com*
2) Type in: 0736821430
3) Click on "FETCH IT" and FactHound will put you on the trail of several helpful links.

You can also search by subject or book title. So, relax and let our pal FactHound do the research for you!

Index